William Bolcom/Arnold Weinstein

Medium Voice and Piano

ANCIENT CABARET

ART SONGS, THAT IS, SONGS ABOUT ART

CONTENTS

I   On a Statue of a Runner 4

II   Unlucky Eutichus 5

III An Encaustic Painting 6

IV   Timomarchus's Picture of Medea, in Rome 8

V   Praxiteles' Aphrodite 10

Recorded on Centaur Records, Inc. CRC2682
William Bolcom and Arnold Weinstein "Cabaret Songs (complete)"
including "Ancient Cabaret"
Joan Morris, mezzo-soprano and William Bolcom, piano
Recorded live at the Flea Theater, New York City

EDWARD B. Marks Music Company

EXCLUSIVELY DISTRIBUTED BY

HAL•LEONARD® CORPORATION

7777 W. BLUEMOUND RD. P.O. BOX 13819 MILWAUKEE, WI 53213

PROGRAM NOTE

The Greek poets were not only artists; many of them were sit-down comics, often making wry and sly comments on their contemporaries. The Palatine Greek anthology of the early Christian era gathered their efforts all the way from the 6th century B.C.E.; these short poems ranged from tough to touching.

—ARNOLD WEINSTEIN

for Joan

Ancient Cabaret
Art Songs, That Is, Songs About Art

Translations from ancient Greek texts
by ARNOLD WEINSTEIN
ANONYMOUS

I. On a Statue of a Runner

WILLIAM BOLCOM
(MMI)

II. Unlucky Eutichus

LUCILIUS

Behold the paint - er Eu - ti - chus

who nev - er got a like - ness once. Not ev - en

from a self - por - trait. Not e - ven from his sev - en sons.

III. An Encaustic Painting

ANONYMOUS

Weirdly tranquil ♩ = 54

I was a cour-te-san _____ in By-zan-tine Rome, All the love that mon-ey could buy. _____ Look at me now in im-mor-tal read-i-ness. My name is

R.H.: very even; *eerie*

u.c. throughout

*In music without key signature, accidentals obtain throughout a beamed group. Unbeamed repeated notes continue the same accidental until interrupted by another note or rest.

IV. Timomarchus's Picture of Medea, in Rome

ANONYMOUS

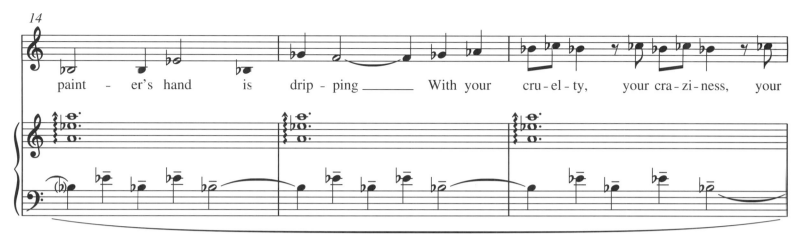

paint - er's hand is drip - ping _____ With your cru - el - ty, your cra - zi - ness, your

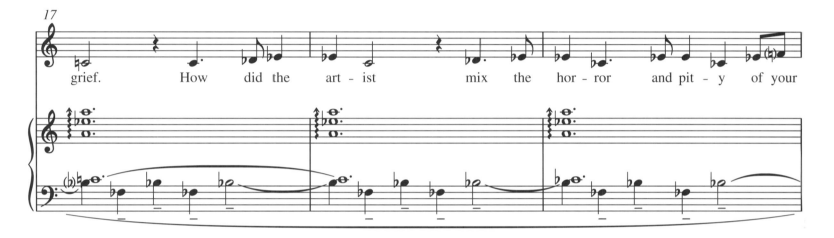

grief. How did the art - ist mix the hor - ror and pit - y of your

Slower

gaze? _____ Blood is thick - er ____ than wa - ter, ___

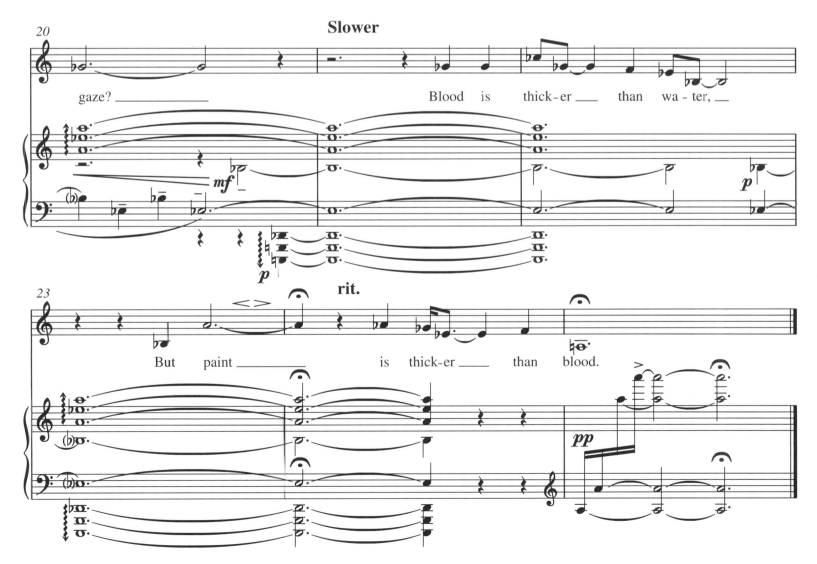

But paint _____ is thick - er ____ than blood.

V. Praxiteles' Aphrodite

PLATO

Capricious, light ♩. = 58

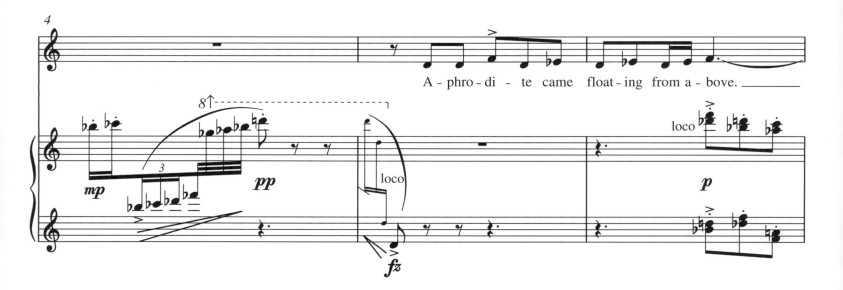

A - phro - di - te came float - ing from a - bove. _____

To see the lat - est sta - tue of her -

self. _____ "This was the

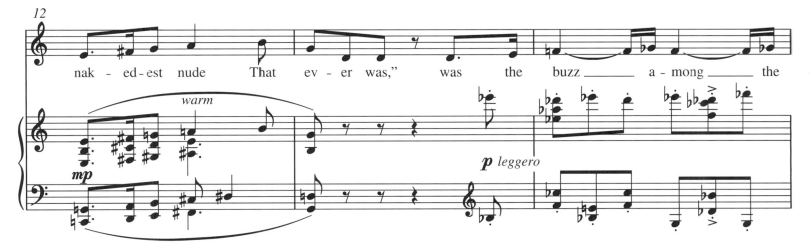

nak - ed - est nude That ev - er was," was the buzz _____ a - mong _____ the

gods. _____ The god - dess looked it up and down,

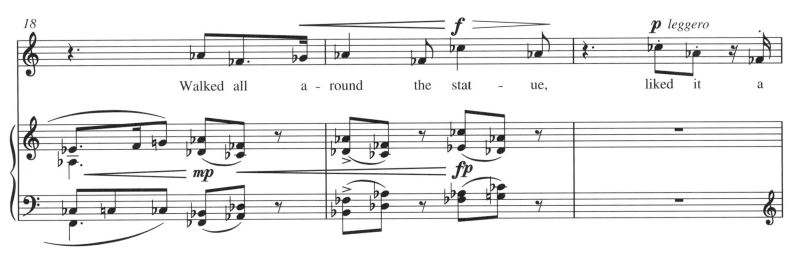

Walked all a - round the stat - ue, liked it a

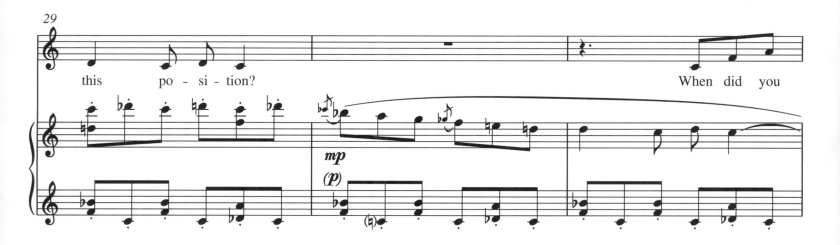

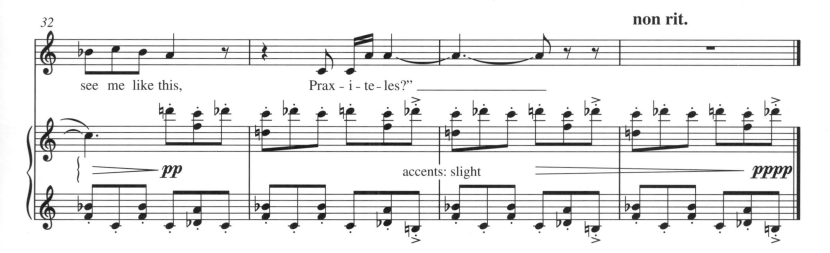